The Open University

AA100
The Arts Past and Present

Illustration Book

Plates for Books 3 and 4

This publication forms part of an Open University course AA100 The Arts Past and Present. Details of this and other Open University courses can be obtained from the Student Registration and Enquiry Service, The Open University, PO Box 197, Milton Keynes MK7 6BJ, United Kingdom: tel. +44 (0)845 300 60 90, email general-enquiries@open.ac.uk

Alternatively, you may visit the Open University website at http://www.open.ac.uk where you can learn more about the wide range of courses and packs offered at all levels by The Open University.

To purchase a selection of Open University course materials visit http://www.ouw.co.uk, or contact Open University Worldwide, Walton Hall, Milton Keynes MK7 6AA, United Kingdom for a brochure. tel. +44 (0)1908 858793; fax +44 (0)1908 858787; email ouw-customer-services@open.ac.uk

Cover image: Paul Cézanne, self-portrait, 1879, oil on canvas. Oskar Reinhart Collection, Winterthur. Photo: akg-images.

The Open University
Walton Hall, Milton Keynes
MK7 6AA

First published 2008

Edited and designed by The Open University.

Typeset by The Open University.

Printed in the United Kingdom by The Westdale Press Limited, Cardiff.

ISBN 9780749217051

1.1

Contents

Book 4   *Place and Leisure*

Plate 3.1.1   Unknown artist, commemorative head of the Queen Mother, Queen Idia, early sixteenth century, Benin, Nigeria, brass, height 39 cm. The British Museum, London, E.T. 1897.10-11.1. Photo: © The Trustees of The British Museum.

Plate 3.1.2 Unknown artist, commemorative head of a king (Oba), Benin, Nigeria, early sixteenth century, brass. The British Museum, London, AOA 1944 Af04.11. Photo: © The Trustees of The British Museum.

Plate 3.1.3 Lorenzo Ghiberti, doors of the Baptistery, Florence, *c*.1430-52, bronze, 506 x 287 cm. Baptistery, Florence. Photo: © 1990 Scala, Florence.

Plate 3.1.4 Unknown artist, head (of Oni, King of Ife?), Ife peoples, Nigeria, twelfth–fourteenth century, bronze, height 36 cm. The British Museum, London, E.T Af1939.34.1. Photo © The Trustees of The British Museum.

Plate 3.1.5 Unknown artist, salt cellar, Benin, Nigeria, sixteenth century, ivory, 31 cm. The British Museum, London, AF 1878.1101.48a-c. Photo: © The Trustees of The British Museum.

Plate 3.1.6   Unknown artist, hunting horn or oliphant, Benin, Nigeria, sixteenth century, ivory. The British Museum, London, AF 1979,1.3158.
Photo: © The Trustees of The British Museum.

Plate 3.1.7 Unknown artist, mask of a queen mother (Idia?), Edo peoples, Benin, Nigeria, sixteenth century, ivory, 25 x 13 x 6 cm. The British Museum, London, Ethno 1910,0513.1. Photo: © The Trustees of The British Museum.

Plate 3.1.8   Unknown artist, relief plaque showing a palace, Benin, Nigeria, sixteenth century, brass. The British Museum, London, Ethno 1898,0115.46. Photo: © The Trustees of The British Museum.

Plate 3.1.9   Unknown artist, relief plaque showing three figures with manilla, Benin, Nigeria, sixteenth century, brass. The British Museum, London, AF,1898,0115,77. Photo: © The Trustees of The British Museum.

Plate 3.1.10   Unknown artist, relief plaque showing a Portuguese soldier or mercenary, Benin, Nigeria, sixteenth century, brass. The British Museum, London, AOA 1928,1.12. Photo: © The Trustees of the British Museum.

Plate 3.1.11　Unknown artist, leopard, Benin, Nigeria, sixteenth century, brass. The British Museum, London, 1949,38.1. Photo: © The Trustees of The British Museum.

Plate 3.1.12 Mausoleum of Maximilian I, 1502-84. Hofkirche, Innsbruck. Photo: Tiroler Landesmuseen. The bronze figures date from 1502 to 1563.

CAPTAIN CAMPBELL'S BRIGADE BRINGING UP THE REAR IN THE ADVANCE ON THE TOWN.

Plate 3.1.13   W.H. Overend, 'Captain Campbell's Brigade Bringing up the Rear in the Advance on the Town', engraving from the *Illustrated London News*, 27 March 1897.

Plate 3.1.14   British officers of the Benin punitive expedition with bronzes and ivories taken from the royal compound, Benin City, 1897. Unknown photographer. British Museum, London, Af-A79.13.
Photo: © Copyright the Trustees of the British Museum.

Plate 3.1.15 Unknown artist, relief plaque showing a warrior with Portuguese men, sixteenth century, brass. The British Museum, London, AF 1898,0115.22. Photo: © The Trustees of The British Museum.

Plate 3.1.16   Unknown artist, relief plaque showing a Portuguese man holding a
manilla, sixteenth century, brass. The British Museum, London,
AF 1899,0710.1. Photo: © The Trustees of The British Museum.

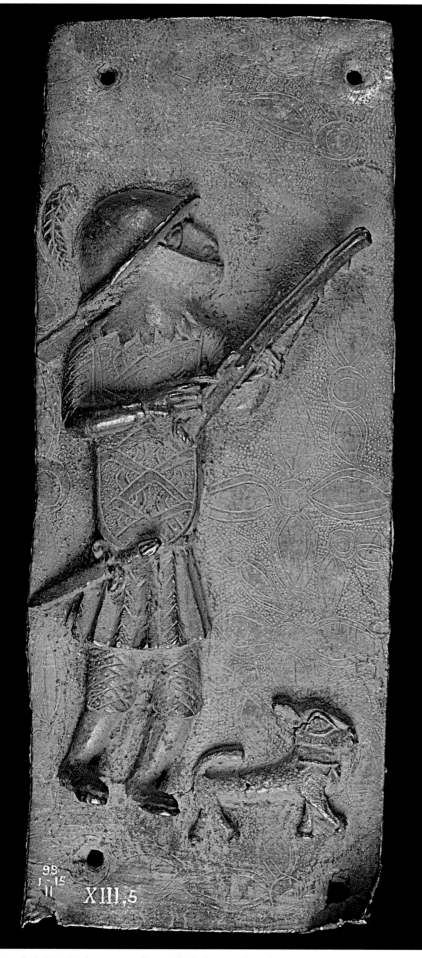

Plate 3.1.17 Unknown artist, relief plaque showing a Portuguese boy hunting
with a dog and musket, sixteenth century, brass. The British Museum, London,
AF 1898,0115.11. Photo: © The Trustees of The British Museum.

Plate 3.1.18 Unknown artist, head, Benin, Nigeria, sixteenth century, bronze. The British Museum, London, AF 1897,1217.3. Photo: © The Trustees of The British Museum.

Plate 3.1.19   Unknown artist, figure playing a side-blown horn, late sixteenth to early seventeenth century, bronze. The British Museum, London, AF 1949,46.156. Photo: © The Trustees of The British Museum.

Plate 3.1.20 Unknown artist, plaque showing a ruler with mud fish legs and leopards, Benin, Nigeria, sixteenth century, brass. British Museum, London, AF1898.0115.29. Photo: © The Trustees of The British Museum.

Plate 3.1.21 Unknown artist, relief plaque showing Oba with two attendants, Benin, Nigeria, sixteenth century, brass. The British Museum, London, Af98,0115.42. Photo: © The Trustees of The British Museum.

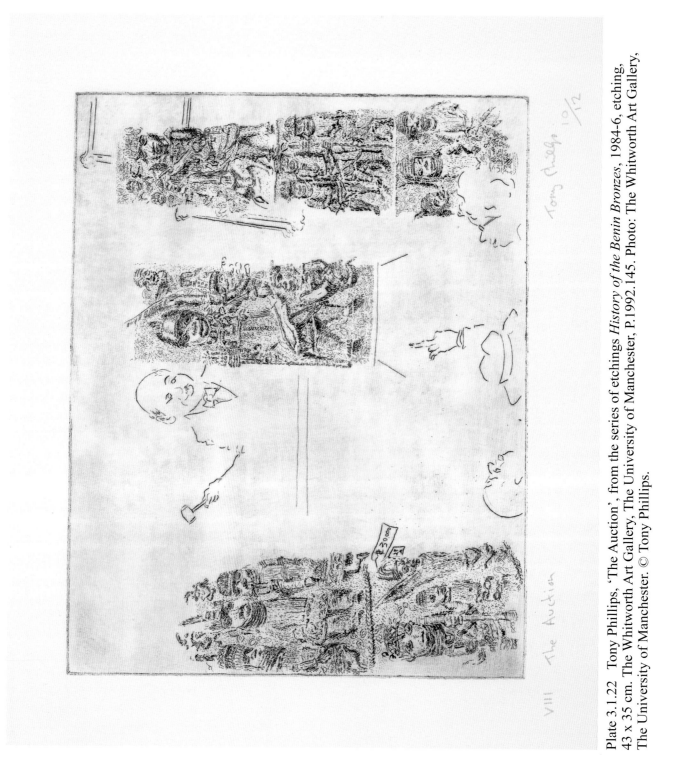

Plate 3.1.22 Tony Phillips, 'The Auction', from the series of etchings *History of the Benin Bronzes*, 1984-6, etching, 43 x 35 cm. The Whitworth Art Gallery, The University of Manchester, P.1992.145. Photo: The Whitworth Art Gallery, The University of Manchester. © Tony Phillips.

Plate 3.1.23   Tony Phillips, 'The Gallery', from the series of etchings *History of the Benin Bronzes*, 1984-6, etching, 43 x 35 cm. The Whitworth Art Gallery, The University of Manchester, P.1992.146. Photo: The Whitworth Art Gallery, The University of Manchester. © Tony Phillips.

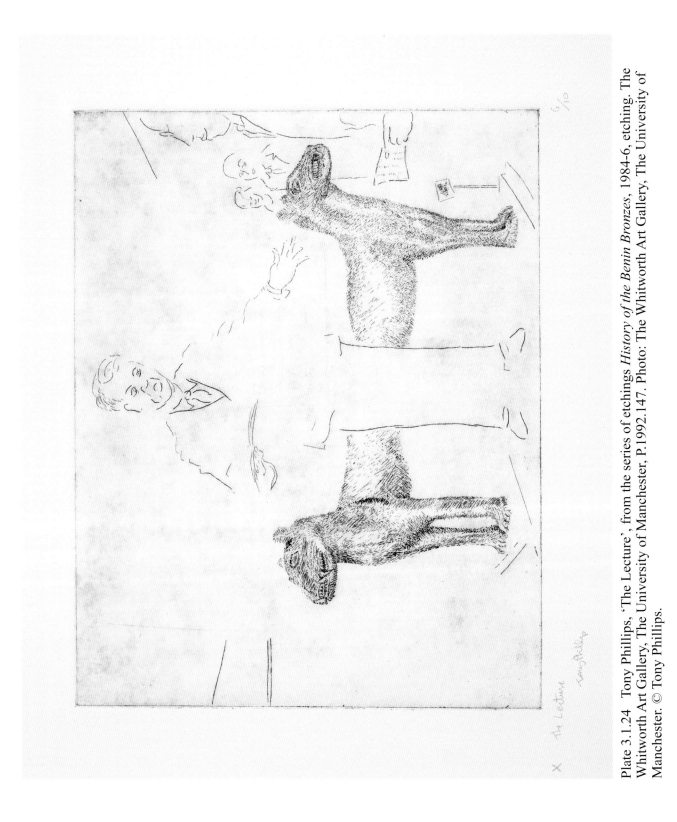

Plate 3.1.24 Tony Phillips, 'The Lecture', from the series of etchings *History of the Benin Bronzes*, 1984-6, etching. The Whitworth Art Gallery, The University of Manchester, P.1992.147. Photo: The Whitworth Art Gallery, The University of Manchester. © Tony Phillips.

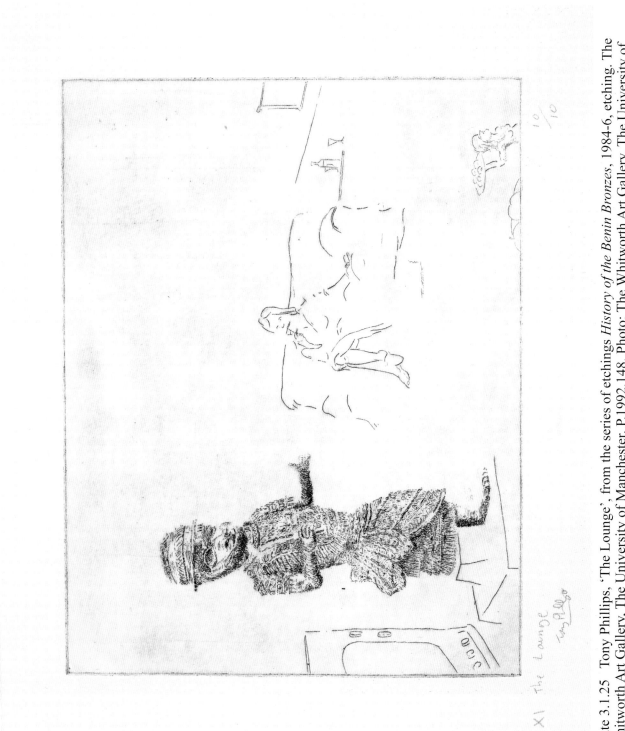

Plate 3.1.25 Tony Phillips, 'The Lounge', from the series of etchings *History of the Benin Bronzes*, 1984-6, etching. The Whitworth Art Gallery, The University of Manchester, P.1992.148. Photo: The Whitworth Art Gallery, The University of Manchester. © Tony Phillips.

Plate 3.2.1 Pablo Picasso, *Les Demoiselles d'Avignon*, 1907, oil on canvas, 238 x 244 cm. Museum of Modern Art, New York. Photo: Lauros / Giraudon/ The Bridgeman Art Library. © Succession Picasso/DACS 2008.

Plate 3.2.2   Paul Gauguin, 'Maruru', 1894–7, woodcut with watercolour, 32 x 23 cm, from *Noa Noa: Tête coupée, guerrier et songe Polynésien*, p. 59. Musée du Louvre, D.A.G. (fonds Orsay), RF7259Folio32recto. Photo: © RMN/Gérard Blot.

Plate 3.2.3 Ernst Ludwig Kirchner, sketch of Palau beams, 1910, pencil, ink and crayon on postcard, 9 x 14 cm. Altonaer Museum, Hamburg, Norddeutsches Landesmuseum. Photo: Altonaer Museum, Hamburg, Norddeutsches Landesmuseum. © Ingeborg & Dr. Wolfgang Henze-Ketterer, Wichtrach/Bern.

Plate 3.2.4   Unknown artist, mask, Fang peoples, Gabon/Republic of Congo, wood and pigment,
48 x 28 x 14 cm. Musée national d'Art moderne – Centre Georges Pompidou, Paris AM1982-248.
Photo: © CNAC/MNAM Dist. RMN/© rights reserved.

Plate 3.2.5 Display of three Fon figures in the Musée d'Éthnographie du Trocadéro, 1895. Unknown photographer. Musée du quai Branly, Paris, archive photograph PP0001264. Photo: © 2008. Musée du quai Branly/Scala, Florence.

Plate 3.2.6   Claude Monet, *Gare St Lazare*, 1877, oil on canvas, 54 x 74 cm. The National Gallery, London. Photo: © The National Gallery, London.

Plate 3.2.7 Ernst Ludwig Kirchner, *Bathers at Moritzburg*, 1909–10, reworked 1926, oil on canvas, 151 x 199 cm. Tate Modern, London, T03067. Photo: Tate, London 2008. © Ingeborg & Dr. Wolfgang Henze-Ketterer, Wichtrach/Bern.

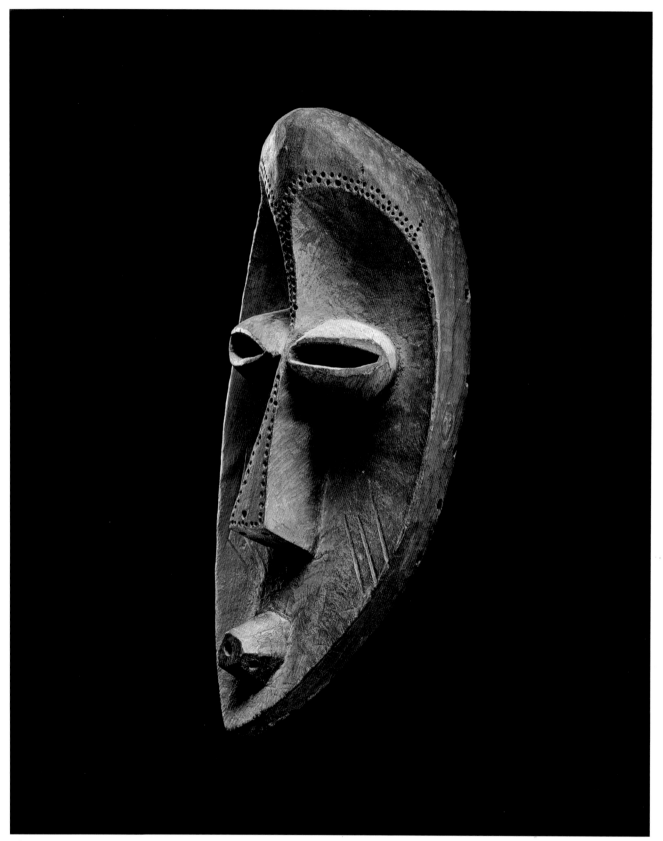

Plate 3.2.8   Unknown artist, mask, Etoumbi region, Republic of Congo, Hongwe or Ngare, polychromed semi-hardwood, height 35 cm. Musée Barbier-Müller, Geneva, inv. 1021-33. Photo: © abm – archives barbier-mueller – studio Ferrazzini-Bouchet, Genève.

Plate 3.2.9   Pablo Picasso, *Seated Nude*, 1909–10, oil on canvas, 92 x 73 cm. Tate Modern, London, N05904. Photo: Tate, London 2008. © Succession Picasso/DACS, 2008.

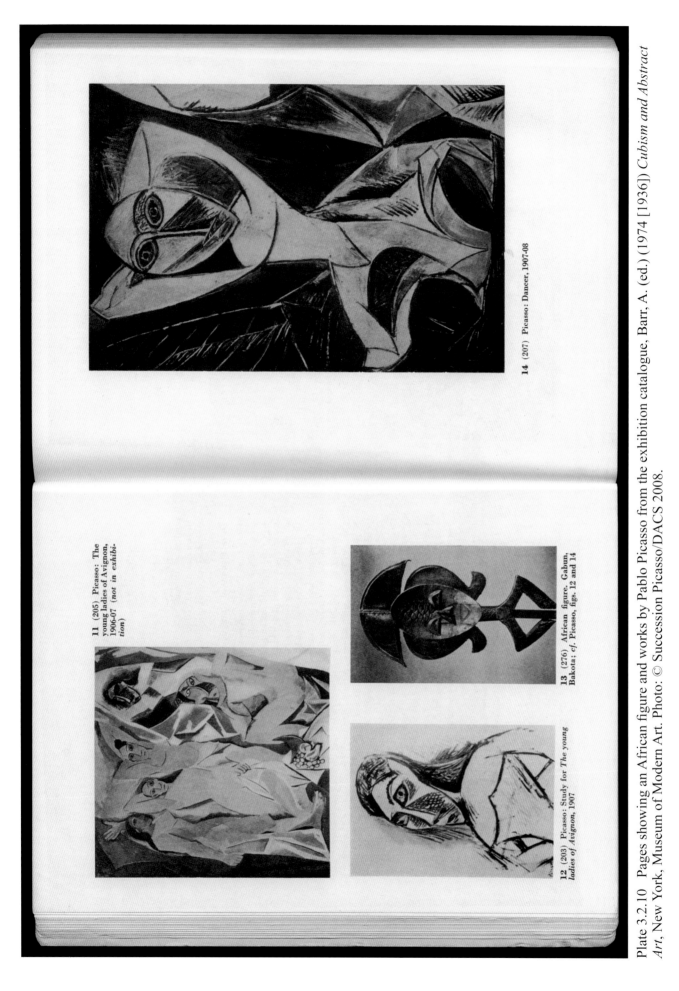

14 (207) Picasso: Dancer, 1907-08

11 (205) Picasso: The young ladies of Avignon, 1906-07 (*not in exhibition*)

13 (276) African figure. Gabun, Bakota; *cf.* Picasso, figs. 12 and 14

12 (203) Picasso: Study for *The young ladies of Avignon*, 1907

Plate 3.2.10 Pages showing an African figure and works by Pablo Picasso from the exhibition catalogue, Barr, A. (ed.) (1974 [1936]) *Cubism and Abstract Art*, New York, Museum of Modern Art. Photo: © Succession Picasso/DACS 2008.

Plate 3.2.11   Unknown artist, mask, Grebo peoples, Ivory Coast, wood, pigment and vegetable fibre, 64 x 26 x 16 cm. Musée Picasso, Paris, MP1983-7. Photo: © RMN/Béatrice Hatala.

Plate 3.2.12 August Rodin, *The Burghers of Calais*, 1908, bronze, 200 x 245 x 231 cm. Victoria Tower Gardens, London. Photo: © Vanni/Art Resource, NY.

Plate 3.2.13   Amadeo Modigliani, *Head*, 1911–12, limestone, 64 x 13 x 35 cm. Tate Modern, London, T03760. Photo: Tate, London 2008.

Plate 3.2.14 Ernst Ludwig Kirchner, *Nude Looking Over Her Shoulder*, 1913, black-dyed oakwood, height 81 cm. Stiftung Museum Kunst Palast, Düsseldorf. Photo: museum kunst palast, Düsseldorf. © Ingeborg & Dr. Wolfgang Henze–Ketterer, Wichtrach/Bern.

Plate 3.2.15 Constantin Brancusi, *Figure and Arch* 1915–16, wood, a work in progress photograph. Musée national d'Art moderne, Centre Georges Pompidou, Paris, archive photograph, PH592B. Photo: © CNAC/ MNAM, Dist. RMN/Philippe Migeat. © ADAGP, Paris and DACS, London 2008.

Plate 3.2.16   Constantin Brancusi, *King of Kings*, *c*.1938 oak, 300 x 48 x 46 cm. Soloman R. Guggenheim Museum, New York, 56.1449. Photo: David Heald. © The Solomon R. Guggenheim Foundation, New York. © ADAGP, Paris and DACS, London 2008.

Plate 3.2.17 Ernst Ludwig Kirchner, *Benin Bronze Sculpture*, 1911, pencil. © Ingeborg & Dr. Wolfgang Henze-Ketterer, Wichtrach/Bern.

Plate 3.2.18   Unknown artist, relief plaque showing an Oba with attendants and Portuguese heads, Benin, Nigeria, sixteenth to seventeenth century, brass, 43 x 40 cm. Staatliche Museum für Völkerkunde, Dresden, inv. 16139. Photo: SES, Staatliche Museum für Völkerkunde, Dresden (MVD)/Eva Winkler.

Plate 3.2.19   Max Pechstein, *Erlegung des Festbratens*, 1912, wood block print, 22.5 x 26 cm.
Foundation Moritzburg, Halle an der Saale, Collection Hermann Gerlinger. Photo: Stiftung Moritzburg,
Landeskunstmuseum Sachsen-Anhalt. © Pechstein Hamburg/Toekendorf / DACS, 2008.

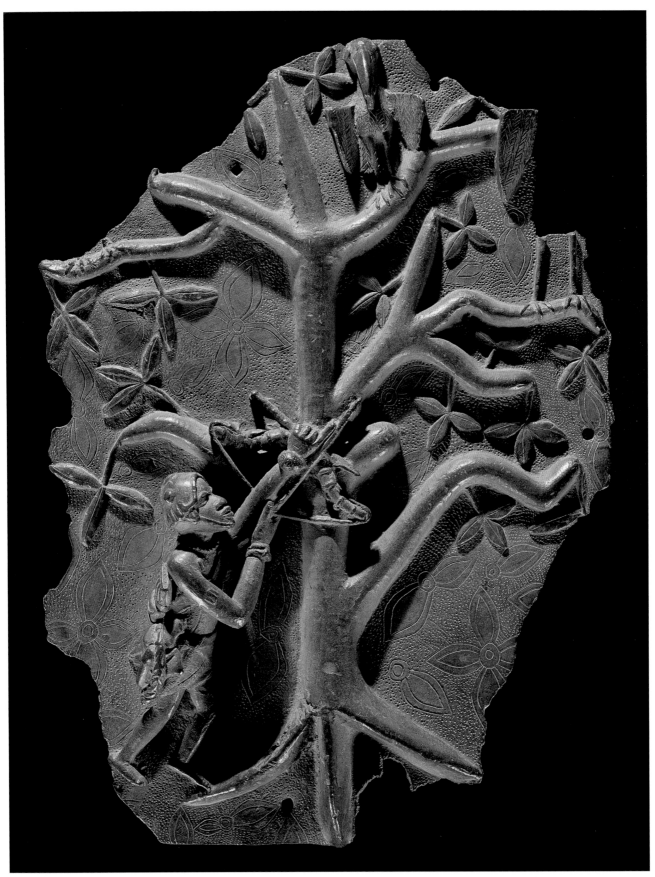

Plate 3.2.20   Master of the Leopard Hunt, relief plaque showing a bird hunt, Benin, Nigeria, brass, 45 x 34 x 5 cm. Ethnologisches Museum – Staatliche Museen zu Berlin, III C 8206. Photo: bpk/Ethnologisches Museum, Staatliche Museen zu Berlin.

Plate 3.2.21   Arsene Matton, *Belgium Brings Civilisation to the Congo*, *c*.1910-22, bronze. Royal Museum for Central Africa, Tervuren, A.333. Photo: Paul Wood.

Plate 3.2.22 General view of the collection, Pitt Rivers Museum, Oxford, c.1904. Unknown photographer. Pitt Rivers Museum, Oxford, archive photograph 1998.267.95.3. Photo: © Pitt Rivers Museum.

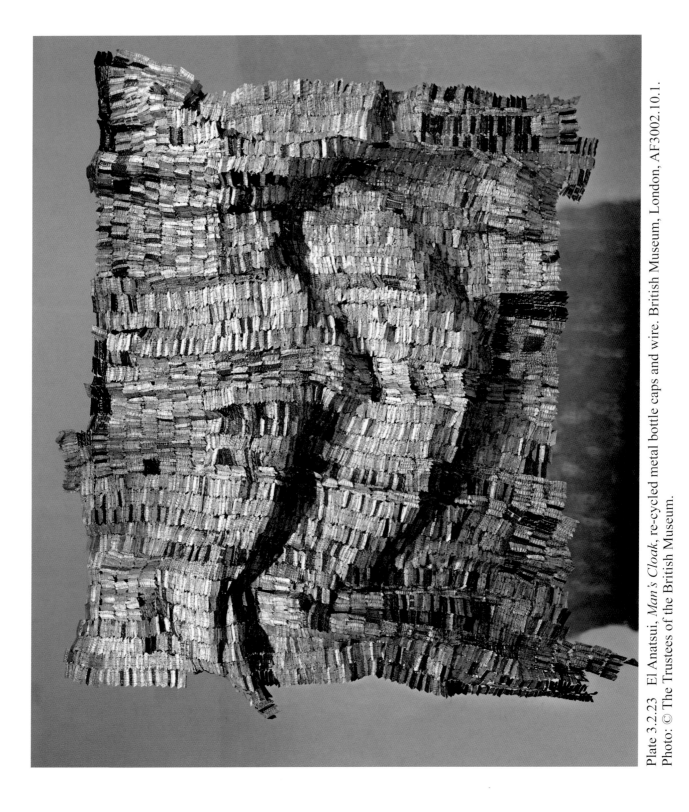

Plate 3.2.23 El Anatsui, *Man's Cloak*, re-cycled metal bottle caps and wire. British Museum, London, AF3002.10.1.
Photo: © The Trustees of the British Museum.

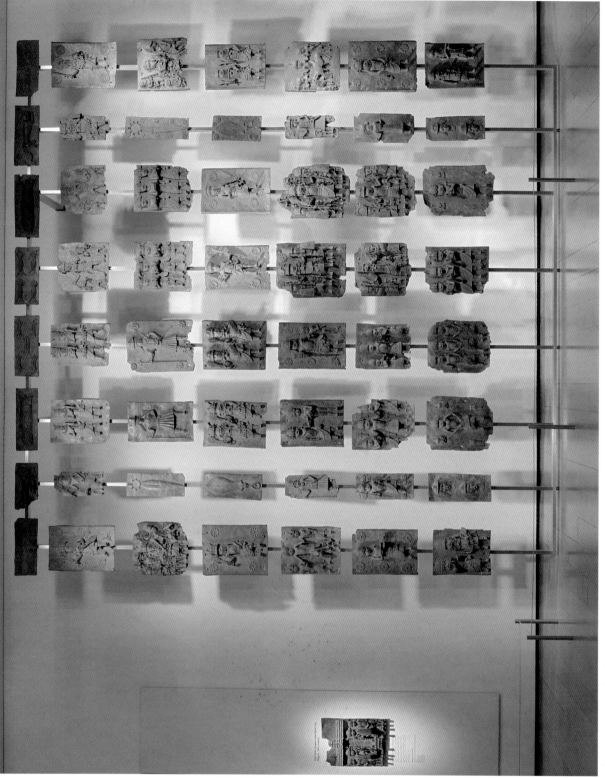

Plate 3.2.24 Display of Benin bronzes in The Sainsbury African Galleries, the British Museum, 2005. Unknown photographer. The British Museum, London, 24041. Photo: © The Trustees of the British Museum.

Plate 3.2.25 Display of Benin bronzes at the Horniman Museum, London, 2007. Unknown photographer. Photo: Horniman Museum.

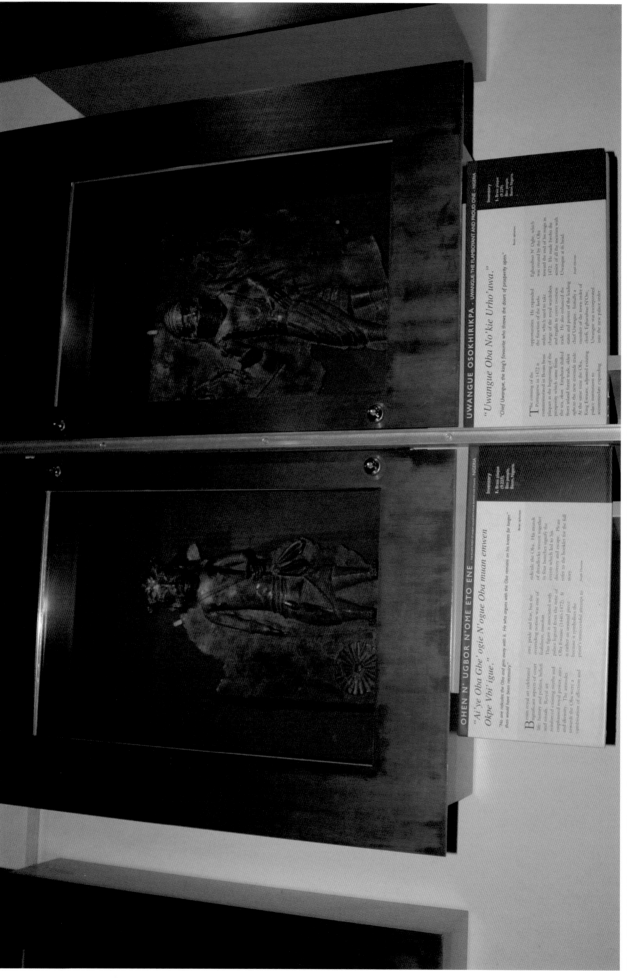

Plate 3.2.26 Display of Benin bronzes at the Horniman Museum, detail, 2007. Unknown photographer. Photo: The Horniman Museum.

Plate 3.2.27   Page showing four sixteenth-century brass plaques from Benin, Nigeria, plate XVIII from Read, C.H. and Dalton, O.M. (1898) 'Works of Art from Benin City', *Journal of the Anthropological Institute*, vol. XXVII, pp. 362–82. The British Library, London, 4698.050000.
Photo: © British Library Board. All rights reserved.

Plate 3.2.28   Unknown artist, relief plaque showing Ezomo Agban, deputy commander in chief of the Benin Army, Benin, Nigeria, nineteenth century, bronze/brass. Horniman Museum, London. Photo: Heini Schneebeli, Horniman Museum.

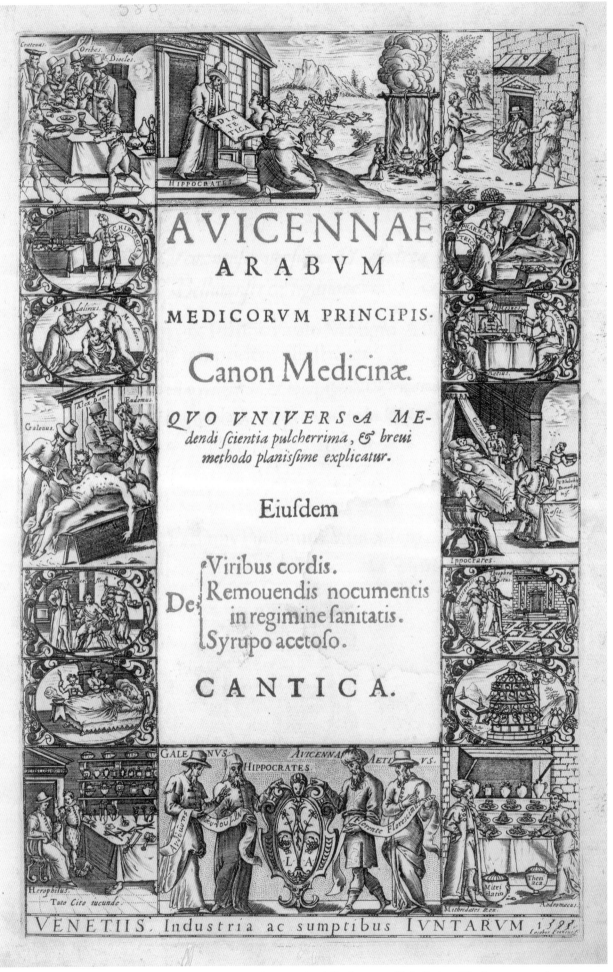

Plate 3.5.1 Unknown artist, title page from Avicenna (1595) *Canon of Medicine*, Venice, engraving.
Wellcome Library, London, 580/D Vol. I. Photo: Wellcome Photo Library.

Plate 3.6.1   The Analatos Painter (attrib.), Attic black figure hydria, water carrying jar for funeral ritual, Geometric (Proto-Attic) period, 700 BCE, fired clay with painted slip decoration, 45 x 29 x 23 cm. National Gallery of Victoria, Melbourne D23-1982 Felton Bequest 1982. Photo: National Gallery of Victoria, Melbourne, Australia.

Plate 3.6.2   The Analatos Painter (attrib.), Attic black figure hydria, water carrying jar for funeral ritual, detail of neck, Geometric (Proto-Attic) period, 700 BCE, fired clay with painted slip decoration, 45 x 29 x 23 cm. National Gallery of Victoria, Melbourne D23-1982 Felton Bequest 1982. Photo: National Gallery of Victoria, Melbourne, Australia.

Plate 3.6.3 Achilles Painter (attrib.), Attic white-ground lekythos (oil flask), showing a woman and a maid taking offerings to the tomb, classical period 460–50 BCE, fired clay with painted slip decoration, 35 x 11 cm diameter. National Gallery of Victoria, Melbourne, D93-1971, Felton Bequest, 1971. Photo: National Gallery of Victoria, Melbourne, Australia.

Plate 3.6.4 Achilles Painter (attrib.), Attic white-ground lekythos (oil flask), showing a woman and a maid taking offerings to the tomb, classical period 460–50 BCE, fired clay with painted slip decoration, 35 x 11 cm diameter. National Gallery of Victoria, Melbourne D93-1971 Felton Bequest, 1971. Photo: National Gallery of Victoria, Melbourne, Australia.

Plate 3.6.5   Sabouroff Painter (attrib.), Attic white-ground lekythos (oil flask) showing the prothesis (laying out of the dead), *c*.450 BCE, terracotta with painted slip decoration, 32 x 10 cm. The Metropolitan Museum of Art, New York, 07.286.40, Rogers Fund, 1907. Photo: © 2002 The Metropolitan Museum of Art.

Plate 3.6.6   Sabouroff Painter (attrib.), Attic white-ground lekythos (oil flask) showing the prothesis (laying out of the dead), *c*.450 BCE, terracotta with painted slip decoration, 32 x 10 cm. The Metropolitan Museum of Art, New York, 07.286.40, Rogers Fund, 1907. Photo: © 2002 The Metropolitan Museum of Art.

Plate 3.6.7 Vouni Painter (attrib.), Attic white-ground lekythos (oil flask) showing a woman and young man either side of two grave stelai bound with fillets, c.460 BCE, terracotta with painted slip decoration, 42 x 14 cm. The Metropolitan Museum of Art, New York, 35.11.5, Purchase, Anonymous Gift, 1935. Photo: 2002 The Metropolitan Museum of Art.

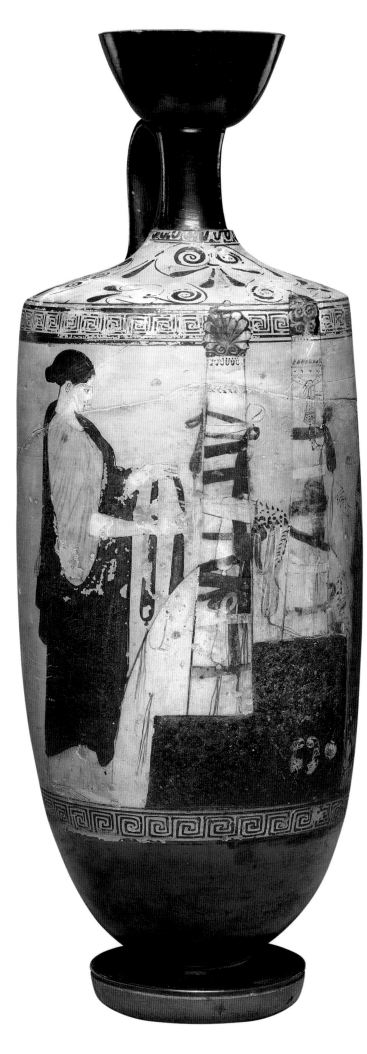

Plate 3.6.8   Vouni Painter (attrib.), Attic white-ground lekythos (oil flask) showing a woman and young man either side of two grave stelai bound with fillets, *c*.460 BCE, terracotta with painted slip decoration, 42 x 14 cm. The Metropolitan Museum of Art, New York, 35.11.5, Purchase, Anonymous Gift, 1935. Photo: 2002 The Metropolitan Museum of Art.

Plate 3.6.9   Near Timocrates Painter (attrib),
Attic white-ground lekythos (oil flask) showing
two women preparing to visit a grave, c.460
BCE, earthenware with painted slip decoration,
38 x 13 cm at shoulder. Chazen Museum of Art,
University of Wisconsin-Madison, 70.2, Edna
G. Dyar Fund and Fairchild Foundation Fund
purchase, 70.2. Photo: Chazen Museum of Art.

Plate 3.6.10 Keening woman in *The Wind that Shakes the Barley*, dir. Ken Loach (Sixteen Films, 2006). Photo: © Sixteen Films.

Plate 3.6.11 Victoria Bradbury, masks created for Gregory McCart's production of Sophokles, *Oidipous the King*, 1995–96, papier mâché. Photo and masks by courtesy of Gregory McCart and the University of Southern Queensland, Australia.

Plate 3.6.12   Pronomos Painter (attrib.), Athenian red-figure volute-krater showing the cast of a satyr play, late fifth century BCE, ceramic with painted slip decoration, height 75 cm. Museo Archeologico Nazionale, Naples, 81673. Photo: Courtesy of Ministero per i Beni e le Attività Culturali.

Plate 3.6.13   Pronomos Painter (attrib.), Athenian red-figure volute-krater showing the cast of a satyr play, late fifth century BCE, ceramic with painted slip decoration, height 75 cm. Museo Archeologico Nazionale, Naples, 81673. Photo: Courtesy of Ministero per i Beni e le Attività Culturali.

Plate 3.6.14   Pronomos Painter (attrib.), Athenian red-figure volute-krater showing the cast of a satyr play, late fifth century BCE, ceramic with painted slip decoration, height 75 cm. Museo Archeologico Nazionale, Naples, 81673. Photo: Courtesy of Ministero per i Beni e le Attività Culturali.

Plate 3.6.15   Pronomos Painter (attrib.), Athenian red-figure volute-krater showing
the cast of a satyr play, late fifth century BCE, ceramic with painted slip decoration,
height 75 cm. Museo Archeologico Nazionale, Naples, 81673. Photo: Courtesy of
Ministero per i Beni e le Attività Culturali.

Plate 3.6.16 The Theatre of Dionysus, Athens, originally fifth century BCE but much reconstructed and restored. Photographed by Hervé Champollion. Photo: © Hervé Champollion/Topp, Camera Press, London.

Plate 3.6.17   Winston Ntshona as Antigone in The Market Theatre production of Athol Fugard, *The Island*, 1995, Johannesburg. Photographed by Ruphin Coudyzer. Photo: © Ruphin Coudyzer FPPSA – www.ruphin.com.

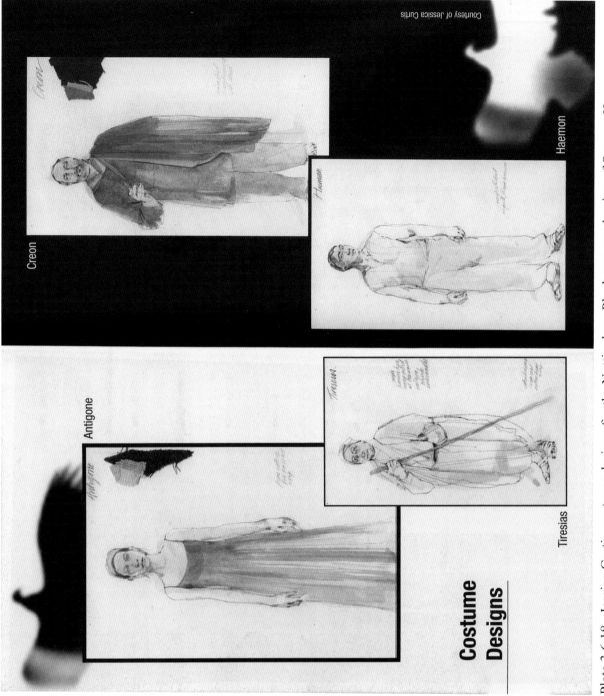

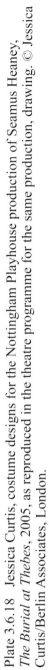

Courtesy of Jessica Curtis

Creon

Haemon

Antigone

Tiresias

Costume Designs

Plate 3.6.18   Jessica Curtis, costume designs for the Nottingham Playhouse production of Seamus Heaney, *The Burial at Thebes*, 2005, as reproduced in the theatre programme for the same production, drawing. © Jessica Curtis/Berlin Associates, London.

Plate 4.2.1 Summer Solstice revellers, Stonehenge, June 2005. Photographed by Matt Cardy. Photo: © Matt Cardy/Alamy.

Plate 4.2.2   Aerial view of Avebury. Photo: © London Aerial Photo Library.

Plate 4.2.3   Jane Brideson, *Wheel of the Year*. © Jane Brideson.

Plate 4.2.4 Chalice Well, Glastonbury Goddess Conference, Glastonbury, August, 2007. Photographed by Marion Bowman.

Plate 4.2.5 Glastonbury Festival with main Pyramid stage and Glastonbury Tor beyond. Photographed by Patrick Ward. Photo: © Patrick Ward/Alamy.

Plate 4.2.6   Glastonbury Tor in the mist, Isle of Avalon. Photographed by David Noton. Photo: © David Noton Photography/Alamy.

Plate 4.2.7　Aerial view of Glastonbury town, 2004. Photographed by Tatu. Photo: © Tatu/Alamy.

Plate 4.2.8   Aerial view of Central Milton Keynes, April 1998. Photographed by Sandy Stockwell.
Photo: © London Aerial Photo Library/CORBIS.

Plate 4.3.1 View of the House of Menander, from Pompeii, *Exedra* 24: the centre of the painted zone, under the stuccoed apse shows a shrine enclosing the figure of Venus. Photo: © Soprintendenza Archeologica di Pompeii. With authorisation of the Ministry for Cultural Heritage and Environment.

Plate 4.3.2   View of the House of Menander, from Pompeii, *Ala* (4): north wall (detail); sack of Troy.
Right: Ajax drags Cassandra away from the Palladion. Left: Menelaus seizes Helen by the hair.
Photograph: © Soprintendenza Archeologica di Pompeii. With authorisation of the Ministry for Cultural
Heritage and Environment.

Plate 4.3.3 View of the House of Menander, from Pompeii, *Ala* (4): east wall (detail); entry of the wooden horse into Troy. Photo: © Soprintendenza Archeologica di Pompeii. With authorisation of the Ministry for Cultural Heritage and Environment.

Plate 4.3.4 View of the House of Menander, from Pompeii, *Exedra* 23: west wall; portrait of Menander (his scroll carries the identification in Latin: 'Menander this man was the first to write New Comedy'). Photo: © Soprintendenza Archeologica di Pompeii. With authorisation of the Ministry for Cultural Heritage and Environment.

Plate 4.3.5   Wall-painting of a seaside villa, from Stabiae, 25 cm in diameter. Museo Archeologico Nazionale, Naples, inv. 9511. Photo: © Soprintendenza per i Beni Archeologici delle province di Napoli e Caserta, MiBAC.

Plate 4.3.6 Wall-painting of a seaside villa, from Stabiae, 40 x 17 cm. Museo Archeologico Nazionale, Naples, inv. 9480. Photo: © Soprintendenza per i Beni Archeologici delle province di Napoli e Caserta, MiBAC.

Plate 4.3.7   Wall-painting of a seaside villa, from Stabiae, 30 x 50 cm. Antiquarium Stabiano inv. 2518. Photo: © Soprintendenza Archeologica di Pompeii. With authorisation of the Ministry for Cultural Heritage and Environment.

Plate 4.3.8 Sacro-idyllic landscape, from Herculaneum, 34 x 61 cm. Museo Archeologico Nazionale, Naples, inv. 9419. Photo: © Soprintendenza per i Beni Archeologici delle province di Napoli e Caserta, MiBAC.

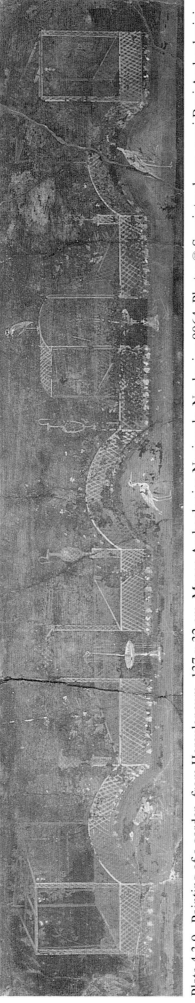

Plate 4.3.9 Painting of a garden, from Herculaneum, 137 x 32 cm. Museo Archeologico Nazionale, Naples inv.9964. Photo: © Soprintendenza per i Beni Archeologici delle province di Napoli e Caserta, MiBAC.

TRANSACTIONS OF THE ROYAL INSTITUTE OF BRITISH ARCHITECTS, 1880-81.

REMAINS OF ROMAN BUILDINGS NEAR BRADING, ISLE OF WIGHT. (N°8)

J.P.Emslie,del.

J.P.& W.R.Emslie, lith.

0 1 2 3 4 5 6   1   2   3   4   5 feet

PAVEMENT IN CHAMBER III.

Plate 4.3.10   Plan of Room 3, Brading Villa, from Price, J.E. and Hilton Price, F.G. (1881) *A description of the remains of Roman buildings at Morton, near Brading, Isle of Wight*, London.

REMAINS OF ROMAN BUILDINGS NEAR BRADING, ISLE OF WIGHT. (Nº 9)

PAVEMENT IN CHAMBER VI.

Plate 4.3.11   Plan of Room 6, Brading Villa, from Price, J.E. and Hilton Price, F.G. (1881) *A description of the remains of Roman buildings at Morton, near Brading, Isle of Wight*, London.

Plate 4.3.12   Plan of Room 12, Brading Villa, from Price, J.E. and Hilton Price, F.G. (1881) *A description of the remains of Roman buildings at Morton, near Brading, Isle of Wight*, London.

97

Plate 4.4.1   William Powell Frith, *Life at the Seaside: Ramsgate Sands*, 1852-4, oil on canvas, 77 x 155 cm. The Royal Collection © 2007 Her Majesty Queen Elizabeth II.

Plate 4.4.2   Charles Landseer, *The Dying Warrior*, 1843–5, oil on canvas, 79 x 99 cm. The Royal Academy of Arts, London. Photo: © Royal Academy of Arts, London.

Plate 4.4.3   William Powell Frith, *Derby Day*, 1856–8, oil on canvas, 102 x 224 cm. Tate Britain, London. Photo: © Tate, London 2007.

Plate 4.4.4 William Powell Frith, *The Railway Station* (Paddingon Station), 1862, oil on canvas, 117 x 256 cm. Royal Holloway College, University of London, Egham. © Royal Holloway and Bedford New College, Surrey/The Bridgeman Art Library.

Plate 4.4.5   Nicholas Poussin, *The Exposition of Moses*, 1654, oil on canvas, 150 x 204 cm. Ashmolean Museum, Oxford.

Plate 4.4.6   Adriaen van de Velde, *The Beach at Scheveningen*, 1658, oil on canvas, 50 x 74 cm. Gemaeldegalerie Alte Meister, Kassel. © Museumslandschaft Hessen Kassel/The Bridgeman Art Library.

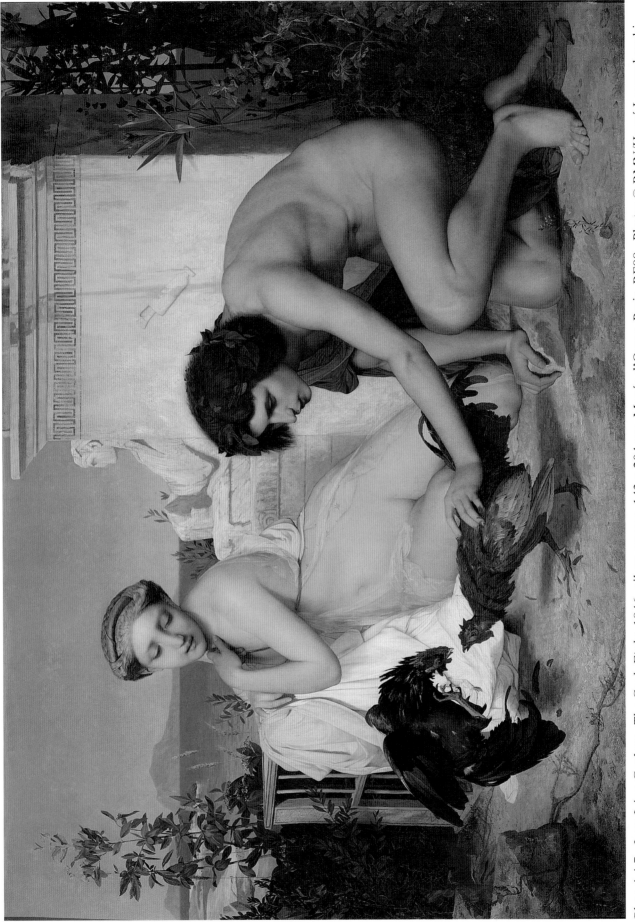

Plate 4.4.7 Jean-Léon Gerôme, *The Cock-Fight*, 1846, oil on canvas, 143 x 204 cm. Musée d'Orsay, Paris, RF88. Photo: © RMN/Hervé Lewandowski.

Plate 4.4.8   Robert Seymour, *Captain and Mrs Waters Greeting the Tuggs Family on Ramsgate Sands*, 1836, engraving. Taken from *The Library of Fiction* by Charles Dickens, Chapman and Hall, London. Houghton Library, Harvard University. Call number: *59s-107. By permission of the Houghton Library, Harvard University.

Plate 4.4.9 Eugène Boudin, *Beach Scene, Trouville. c.*1860–70, oil on wood, 22 x 46 cm. National Gallery, London, NG 6309. © National Gallery, London. Bequeathed by Miss Judith E. Wilson, 1960.

Plate 4.4.10   Eugène Boudin, *Bathing Time at Deauville*, 1865, oil on wood, 35 x 58 cm.   National Gallery of Art, Washington.   Collection of Mr and Mrs Paul Mellon. Image courtesy of the Board of Trustees, National Gallery of Art, Washington.

Plate 4.4.11 Eugene Isabey, *The Beach at Granville*, 1863, oil on canvas, 83 x 124 cm. Musée du Vieux-Château, Laval. Photo: Cliché Leportier

Plate 4.4.12 Claude Monet, *Beach at Trouville*, 1870, oil on canvas, 38 x 46 cm. National Gallery, London, NG3951. © The National Gallery, London. Bought by the Trustees of the Courtauld Fund, 1924.

Plate 4.4.13 Claude Monet, *The Beach at Trouville*, 1870, oil on canvas, 48 x 74 cm. Private collection. Photo courtesy of Sotheby's Picture Library.

Plate 4.4.14   Walter Richard Sickert, *Bathers, Dieppe*, 1902, oil on canvas, 132 x 104 cm. Walker Art Gallery, Liverpool, WAG2262. Photo: © National Museums Liverpool, Walker Art Gallery.

Plate 4.4.15 Philip Wilson Steer, *Walberswick, Children Paddling*, c.1889-94, oil on canvas, 64 x 92 cm. Fitzwilliam Museum, Cambridge. © Fitzwilliam Museum, University of Cambridge/The Bridgeman Art Library. © Tate, London 2007.

Plate 4.4.16   Edouard Manet, *On the Beach at Boulogne-sur-Mer*, 1869, oil on canvas, 32 × 65 cm. Virginia Museum of Fine Arts, Richmond. Collection of Mr and Mrs Paul Mellon. Photo: Katherine Wetzel, © Virginia Museum of Fine Arts.

Plate 4.4.17 Eugene le Poittevin, *Sea-Bathing at Etretat*, 1866, oil on canvas, 66.5 x 152 cm. Musée des Beaux-Arts, Troyes. Association Peindre en Normandie, Caen/The Bridgeman Art Library.

Plate 4.4.18 Edouard Manet, *Sur la Plage*, 1873, oil on canvas, 60 x 73 cm. Musée d'Orsay, Paris, RF1953-24. © Photo RMN/Hervé Lewandowski.

Plate 4.4.19 Edgar Degas, *Beach Scene*, oil on canvas, 48 x 83 cm. National Gallery, London NG 3247. © National Gallery, London. Lane Bequest, 1917.

Plate 4.4.20   Edvard Munch, *Melancholy*, 1891, oil on canvas, 72 x 98 cm. Bergen Art Museum, The Rasmus Meyer Collection.
Photo: Werner Zellien. © Munch Museum/Munch, Ellingsen Group, BONO, Oslo/DACS, London 2008.

Plate 4.4.21 Christopher Wood, *The Plage, Hotel Ty-Mad, Tréboul*, 1930, oil on board, 46 x 55 cm. Sheffield Art Galleries. © Sheffield Galleries and Museums Trust/The Bridgeman Art Library.

Plate 4.4.22 Buckets and Spades, 1890. Photographed by F.J. Mortimer. Photo: Hulton Archive/Getty Images.

The Sands, Margate. 1720. W & D. Lord

Plate 4.4.23 Crowds on Margate Beach, 1890–1910. Unknown photographer. Photo: © English Heritage/NMR.

Plate 4.4.24 Donkey Riders, Blackpool, 1903. Photographed by Rischgitz. Photo: Hulton Archive/Getty Images.

Plate 4.4.25 Unknown artist, poster advertising Blackpool for the Midland Railway, c.1893, 101 x 63 cm. Photo: National Railway Museum/Science & Society Picture Library.

Plate 4.4.26 Blackpool Illuminations, 1912. Unknown photographer. From the collection of Ted Lightbown.

Plate 4.4.27   Blackpool Illuminations, mid twentieth century. Unknown photographer. From the collection of Fred Gray, taken from his book *Designing the Seaside: Architecture, Society and Nature*, London, 2006.

Hotel Canfali   *A street in Benidorm*

Hotel Planesia

THE HOTELS
CANFALI

This lovely and spacious hotel is a veritable sun-trap. Situated on cliffs overlooking the beaches to which there is a direct approach by private stairs. A very beautiful, lofty lounge, sun terraces, and the amenities of private bath or shower in the rooms, a well appointed restaurant and a distinguished atmosphere make the Canfali specially attractive. Many of the rooms have sea view. Other rooms overlook the charming lanes and a square of Old Benidorm.

VICTORIA

One of the best managed hotels in Benidorm, situated in a quiet residential position. All double rooms with private bath and shower, w.c., and balcony; single rooms with shower. Wonderful cuisine, spacious lounges and charming cosy bar. Private swimming-pool.

PLANESIA

This hotel is in the most commanding position on the promontory of "Old Benidorm", right over the cliffs towering above the sea. From its lounge, its bar and its magnificent restaurant you have panoramic views of the beaches and the sea, so you have the feeling of being on board a luxury liner. All the rooms have a private bath, shower, w.c., as well as a private terrace. Most of the rooms overlook the sea. This 1st class "A" hotel is a real joy to experience. Lift to all floors.

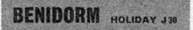

BENIDORM HOLIDAY J30

TRAVEL ARRANGEMENTS AND COSTS

A fortnight's fully inclusive holiday

HOTEL CANFALI
(Price includes private bath, shower and w.c.)

	£ s. d.
Departures on May 19, 26; Sept. 22	51 16 0
Departures on June 2, 9, 16, 23, 30; July 7, 14; Sept. 15	53 16 0
Departures on July 21, 28; Aug. 4, 11, 18, 25; Sept. 1, 8	55 16 0

Supplement: Double rooms with private terrace and sea-view £3 per person. No single rooms available.

HOTEL VICTORIA
(Price includes private bath or shower, w.c. and balcony for double rooms)

Departures on May 19, 26; Sept. 22	54 12 0
Departures on June 2, 9, 16, 23, 30; July 7, 14; Sept. 15	56 12 0
Departures on July 21, 28; Aug. 4, 11, 18, 25; Sept. 1, 8	58 12 0

Supplement: Single rooms with private shower £2.

HOTEL PLANESIA
(Price includes private shower and w.c. for double rooms)

Departures on May 19, 26; Sept. 22	60 2 0
Departures on June 2, 9, 16, 23, 30; July 7, 14; Sept. 15	62 2 0
Departures on July 21, 28; Aug. 4, 11, 18, 25; Sept. 1, 8	64 2 0

Supplement: Double rooms with bath, shower, w.c., terrace and sea-view £3 per person. No single rooms available.

Subject to Government Approval

SUNDAY MORNING DEPARTURES
TO VALENCIA
BY VISCOUNT OF
BRITISH UNITED AIRWAYS
and onward by private coach
to your hotel.

FLYING TIME: 3 hrs. 15 mins.

Take-off Gatwick Airport	3.40 p.m.
Return landing (Sun. fortnight later)................	11.35 p.m.

Full instructions for your journey will be sent to you with your tickets.

Plate 4.4.28   A page featuring Benidorm from Horizon's brochure, 1963.

Plate 4.4.29   Picture postcard view of the South Shore Baths, Blackpool. Unknown photographer. From the collection of John Walton.

Plate 4.4.30 Ocean Dome, Phoenix Seagaia Resort, Miyazaki, Japan. © TW Photos/Corbis.

Plate 4.4.31 Septimus E Scott, poster for New Brighton and Wallasey/London, Midland and Scottish Railway (LMS), 1923.
© Science and Society Picture Library/NRM, Pictorial Collection.

Plate.4.32   Ralph Mott, *Spring*, poster advertising Blackpool for the London, Midland and Scottish Railway (LMS), *c*.1935. © Science and Society Picture Library/NRM, Pictorial Collection.

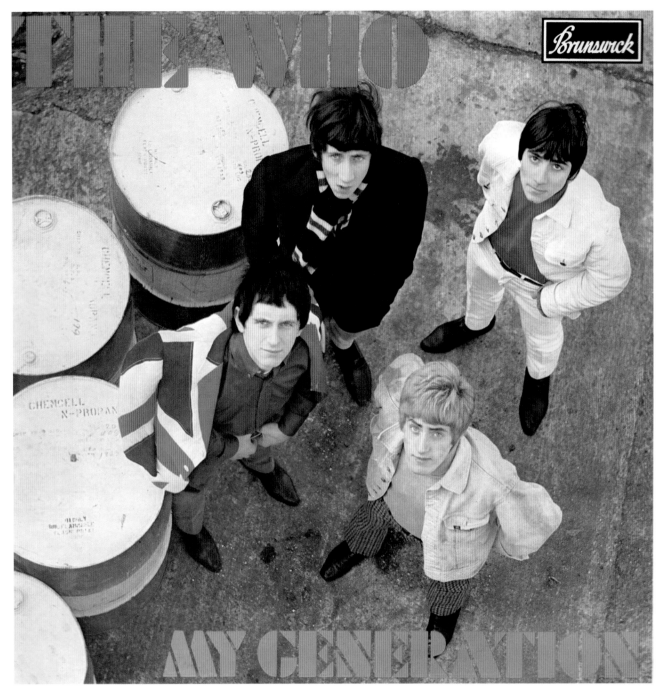

Plate 4.4.33   David Wedgbury, cover of The Who's album *My Generation*, 1965. Sleeve reproduced courtesy of Polydor Limited.

Plate 4.4.34   Graham Hughes, front cover of The Who's album *Quadrophenia*, 1973. Sleeve reproduced courtesy of Polydor Limited.

Plate 4.4.35   Ethan A. Russell, back cover of The Who's album *Quadrophenia*, 1973. Sleeve reproduced courtesy of Polydor Limited.

Plate 4.4.36 Ethan A. Russell, 'Band Members of The Who leaving Hammersmith Odeon with "fans" watched on by the Kid', from the *Quadrophenia* LP booklet, 1973. Sleeve reproduced courtesy of Polydor Limited.

Plate 4.4.37 Ethan A. Russell, 'Breakfast Scene featuring the Kid and his parents', from the *Quadrophenia* LP booklet, 1973. Sleeve reproduced courtesy of Polydor Limited.

Plate 4.4.38   Ethan A. Russell, 'The Kid and Brighton Pier', from the *Quadrophenia* LP booklet, 1973. Sleeve reproduced courtesy of Polydor Limited.

Plate 4.4.39   Ethan A. Russell, 'The Kid in a boat', from the *Quadrophenia* LP booklet, 1973.   Sleeve reproduced courtesy of Polydor Limited.

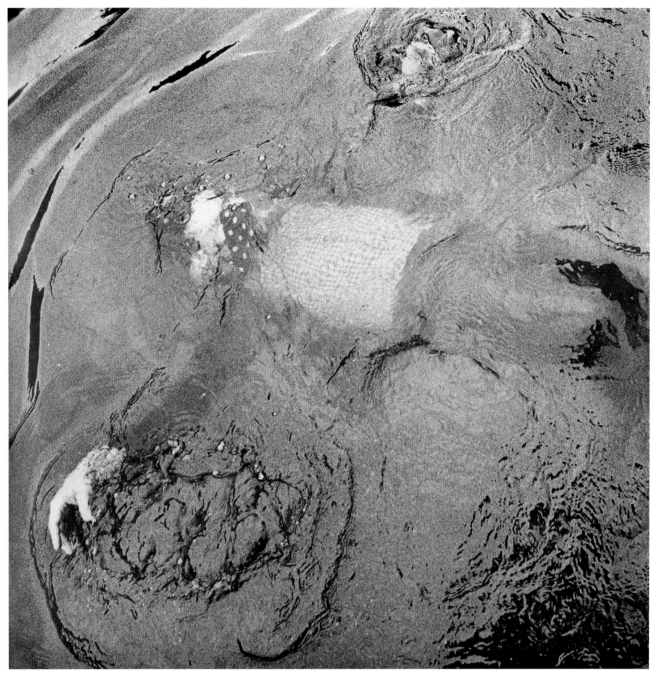

Plate 4.4.40   Ethan A. Russell, 'The Kid underwater', from the *Quadrophenia* LP booklet, 1973. Sleeve reproduced courtesy of Polydor Limited.

Plate 4.4.41 Ethan A. Russell, 'The Kid and the Rock, front view', from the *Quadrophenia* LP booklet, 1973. Sleeve reproduced courtesy of Polydor Limited.

Plate 4.4.42   Ethan A. Russell, 'The Rock, rear view of the Kid', from the *Quadrophenia* LP booklet, 1973. Sleeve reproduced courtesy of Polydor Limited.